THE MYSTERIOUS WORLD OF TIGERS

This title is part of a series of books entitled
ESSENTIAL INDIA EDITIONS. Each book in the series will explore a
foundational aspect of the country in new and thought-provoking ways.

~

THE MYSTERIOUS WORLD OF TIGERS

A BOOK OF DISCOVERY

Valmik Thapar

ALEPH

ALEPH

ALEPH BOOK COMPANY
An independent publishing firm
promoted by *Rupa Publications India*

First published in India in 2025
by Aleph Book Company
161-B/4, Gulmohar House,
Yusuf Sarai Community Centre,
New Delhi 110049

ISBN: 978-93-6523-724-5

1 3 5 7 9 10 8 6 4 2

This book is dedicated to Fateh Singh Rathore, who dedicated his life to building Ranthambhore, and G. V. Reddy, an exceptional forest officer who sustained Ranthambhore at the turn of the century when a crisis engulfed it.

I also dedicate this book to Peter Lawton, who did his best for the future of Ranthambhore, and Aditya Dicky Singh who, after the turn of this century, captured the brilliance of wild tigers with his incredible pictures.

CONTENTS

AUTHOR'S NOTE

*T*his little book reflects some very special moments that I have experienced with wild tigers. It also captures the essence of tigers, and their physiology and abilities.

I came under the spell of the tiger about fifty years ago and have never looked back. The tiger changed my life and took me into a realm of the natural world I would never have believed possible. I have now worked on more than forty-two books, mainly on tigers and Indian wildlife. Every exceptional encounter led to new ideas and a publication. You are forever a student of the tiger and the knowledge keeps growing. I served the tigers and campaigned for them. I talked about them all over the world and presented dozens of international films on their lives. Why? For me, there was nothing more important to do in my life. I was, after all, privileged to see the intimate world of the tiger.

When I first went to Ranthambhore, it was impossible to see tigers. Maybe momentary glimpses at night. It took me years to just see a tiger in the day, drinking water. Fateh Singh Rathore, my tiger guru, worked tirelessly to resettle more than a dozen villages inside the core of this area so the thirteen or fourteen tigers which lived there at the time could find some peace to survive, mate, and rear their young. Today, what was only 400 square kilometres in size, is 1,700 square kilometres and is linked to three other tiger reserves that, together, provide a nearly contiguous habitat of 4,000 square kilometres. And, this area houses just under 100 tigers, a nearly seven-fold increase, the result of the hard work of many dedicated people. To achieve this feat of tiger conservation in five decades is a success story that deserves to be celebrated. I would never have thought it possible. Now, thousands visit the area and mostly see tigers. In the recent past, seeing eight tigers in one outing was not uncommon.

I hope this book, a glimpse into the mysterious world of tigers, one of the world's most charismatic mammals, will help readers understand just how special they are and support efforts to conserve them, and, more broadly, save the environment.

Enjoy!

Valmik Thapar
New Delhi
April 2025

1

RANTHAMBHORE,
MY TIGER HEARTLAND

$\mathcal{I}$ first came under the tiger's spell over fifty years ago, at the age of ten, sitting astride an elephant in Corbett National Park in the Lower Himalaya of North India. It was early in the morning and ten elephants were sweeping through high grass in an attempt to spring some tigers into a clearing on the far side. I remember looking down from my perch and seeing a tigress snarling up at the elephant and then darting away with two large cubs at her heels. I was struck by that experience and continue to remember it vividly. It was thirteen years after this encounter that I saw my next tiger in Ranthambhore National Park in Rajasthan. The year was 1976. That was the year my life with tigers truly began.

Late one afternoon, in early 1976, I boarded a train in Delhi for the small town of Sawai Madhopur, the station I would need to get off at to make my way to the tiger reserve in Ranthambhore. I was a city boy and unsure of what lay ahead. All I knew at that time, at the age of twenty-three, was that something was missing in my life. There was a sense of emptiness and despair, and a lack of excitement. I needed a break. I had heard of Ranthambhore through my work on various documentary films but could not have imagined then that I would find

3

the lure of the jungle irresistible. I remember that that train journey was one of the most difficult that I have ever taken. Instinctively, I must have known that my life was about to change. I watched the dusty plains rush past as the train sped on and soon it was pitch dark. When I disembarked at 10 p.m., I found myself at a station that was dark and deserted. I somehow managed to wake up the driver of a horse carriage that was standing outside. In those days, Sawai Madhopur did not boast many jeeps or motorized vehicles. We trotted off to the only hotel nearby—the Maharaja Lodge—where I had to wake the watchman who took his own sweet time to open up a room festooned with cobwebs for me. I spent a sleepless night. The next morning I set off for a walk and was surprised to see that there was no sign of a forest nearby. This was a sleepy district town sprawled untidily around the railway track, which seemed to be the only reason for its existence. I walked around amidst hooting train sounds and felt people staring at me. I must have seemed like an alien. I began to wonder whether there really were any tigers in the area. Soon, I found another horse cart that would take me to the office of Project Tiger, a government initiative launched in 1973 to conserve the Bengal tiger in India. The office turned out to be a dismal building in the middle of a mess of concrete and brick that is the hallmark of every small town in India. A cement factory nearby belched out dirty smoke. Could this be the base for a tiger reserve?

I introduced myself to Fateh Singh Rathore, the wildlife warden of the park, at the barrack-like office. He looked like someone straight out of the American Wild West with his luxuriant moustache and stetson. I asked his permission to spend some time in the park and he looked me up and down as if I was mad. He told me that no one came there to 'visit' and that I would have to find a jeep and get my rations if I was to stay inside. Not expecting this, I grew a little anxious, but a few hours later I managed to hire a jeep and borrowed Fateh's driver, Prahlad, to set off for the park. The rations had been bought and I had also taken a crate of Coca-Cola along. At the time, Coke was my favourite drink.

Leaving the town, we followed a narrow tarred road that ran parallel to a range of hills and after several kilometres, turned off onto a dirt track. Slowly the wilderness started taking over and the forest thickened. Suddenly, we were skimming along the rim of a deep ravine, bouncing and jolting over a stony track. In front of us loomed an ancient massive stone gate that must have once been flanked by fortress walls, long since crumbled. It was the royal entrance to Ranthambhore, constructed to protect the domain of kings and surviving today to protect a treasure of equal if not greater value. Centuries ago, it must have prevented armies from invading this kingdom. Water flowed down the edge of the gate from a marble cow's head encompassed by a Shivling. A pool of water full of slithery water snakes had formed below the gate; as we moved beyond it, the air cooled and the vegetation changed. So did the sounds, as the chatter of birds mixed incongruously with the groan of the jeep. It is truly amazing how birds are able to survive wherever there is a patch of forest and fill our senses with their song. Cresting a rise, we saw Ranthambhore Fort, grey and enormous, extending upwards from a steep cliff face. The sky was a clear blue, the surrounding forest a dull green just turning to yellow. The huge walls glinted in the evening sunlight, looking for all the world as if man had decided to chisel a bit of nature out of the upper fringe of the rock, rather than disturb or fight it.

The fort was vital for the control of central India, and the great Mughal emperor Akbar laid siege to it in the sixteenth century. In fact, he camped at the fort for a year before taking control. During that time, there are records of battles and intrigue, and the politics of the warring groups but no record of hunts. But I am sure Akbar hunted in the plains with his cheetahs racing after herds of blackbuck. It is likely that tigers were also hunted. It is said that, during Akbar's time, one of the unusual ways to hunt the tiger was by riding a big male buffalo towards it and then controlling the buffalo such that it tossed the tiger to the ground with its horns. Another unconventional method described is that of tying a bait on a path regularly used by tigers and pouring strong glue around the bait. The tiger would then get stuck to the ground and would lose its energy in the struggle to free himself from the glue. But the greatest tiger story from Emperor Akbar's time is one that is considered one of his miracles. He confronted a tiger and looked at it so ferociously that it submitted in front of the emperor, turned, and ran away!

Much later, in 1754, Mughal emperor Shah Alam II issued a firman granting Ranthambhore Fort to Sawai Madho Singh of Jaipur, making him the qiladar or governor of the fort. A traveller of those times described the fort as being one of the most famous in India, well-protected, completely inaccessible, and concealed in a mountainous region; surrounded on all sides by high ridges, leaving the thick forest gorges below to serve as entrances and exits as these could be easily defended. Only cannons could blast the walls down and force entry into the fort; the notorious inaccuracy of cannon fire of the time meant that the fort justified its reputation as being unconquerable. Towers and bastions were built into the walls and the natural rock faces, which added to the fortifications. The rocks on the edges of the ridges constituted another disadvantage for an invading army. These fortifications meant that the occupants of Ranthambhore would suffer only if the fort was under siege. That was why Akbar spent a year laying siege to the fort; and this reality is also revealed by the paintings of those times.

By the turn of the twentieth century, the forests of Ranthambhore became the private hunting reserves of the maharajas of Jaipur. This probably slowed down the destruction of both the forest and the tiger, as the maharajas' men started protecting them. Shooting was permitted only for special guests. A one-month-long shooting camp would be held in Sawai Madhopur and most of the shoots were around the town where the forest spilt over. The hunts are described in great detail by Colonel Kesri Singh in his book, *The Tiger of Rajasthan*. The guests included royalty and nobility from all over Europe, and a number of maharajas from all over India. Kesri Singh managed the shoots well without depleting the forests. The last major shoot was held for the Queen of England and the Duke of Edinburgh in 1961.

I thought about everything I had read about Ranthambhore as we began to wind our way up the road that ran along the right flank of the fort. The forest had grown very dense. We would soon be at our destination. I strained to see through the trees for signs of wildlife, but my eyes were not yet accustomed to seeing in the forest. I did not know then that it would take years for that skill to develop. I could see old peepul trees and large banyans, and I wondered how much they had changed since Ranthambhore's glory days. As we crested another rise, the terrain changed dramatically. The steep hills gave way to a broad valley dotted with low hills and a large expanse of water clothed entirely in giant pink and white lotuses. The colour of the blooms resembled the pink of lotus flowers that dotted the cloth paintings or Pichhwais from the area of Nathdwara near Udaipur, a pink that I had never before believed possible to encounter in real life. It was too much to assimilate all at once, this mix of history, man, and nature.

As we branched to the left, I thought we were plunging into the largest banyan tree I had ever seen. Two of its hundreds of roots formed a natural gateway to Jogi Mahal, the forest rest house, which decades ago had been the residence of a temple priest. Before the driver could even stop, I raced up the steps across a wide terrace and through a high arched doorway to an awe-inspiring view. There at my feet lay the lake of lotuses that I had glimpsed earlier, with the waters of the lake lapping peacefully against the base of the rest house. In the distance crocodiles lay sunbathing, one with its jaw open, another gliding lazily through the water. Wild boar, chital, and sambar fed on the lush grass on the bank of the lake. Some of the sambar were half immersed in the water, nibbling at the lotus leaves. Darters, herons, grebes, and kingfishers were flying around in abandon. Occasionally, a large fish would breach the surface of the lake and fall back into the water with a loud, slapping noise. To the right of the lake were the remnants of an old masjid and upon the opposite hill was an ancient guard post. On the other side were the vast banyan tree and the backdrop of Ranthambhore Fort, which filled the horizon with its imposing presence. It was a moment of hypnotic intensity for me and I was suddenly exhausted. This is where I would stay. I did not know then that Ranthambhore would become more like home for about a half-century and a place that would always regenerate my soul.

2

A TIGER FAMILY

$\mathscr{A}$fter an exciting four weeks in Ranthambhore, looking for the elusive tiger and getting to know Fateh Singh, I was back in Delhi, remembering and savouring my rousing first encounter with a tiger in the reserve. I went back to Ranthambhore a couple of times that year and each visit whetted my appetite for more. In Delhi, I would spend every day waiting in keen anticipation for exciting news from Ranthambhore. It came soon enough with the new year—1977. The doorbell rang—there was a telegram for me, from Fateh Singh. 'Come immediately,' it said. In a mad rush, my brother-in-law, Tejbir Singh, and I organized ourselves to leave in the morning. We took the train and were met by an excited and jumpy Fateh at the other end. His first words (and I still remember them) were, 'A tigress has been spotted with five cubs.' Fateh Singh then spent some time explaining. His experience had begun several months ago when he first set eyes on the tigress, whom we now decided to name Padmini.

The year in which her story starts is 1976. Padmini was then a nearly five-year-old tigress in Ranthambhore and Fateh Singh sighted her in a very pregnant state, her belly bulging hugely. This is cause for great excitement to any field man in a forest: a new lot of tiger cubs to be born.

Driving his jeep near the vacated Lakarda village on an evening in December 1976, he sighted some pugmarks. A careful examination of the tracks immediately revealed that a tigress was moving with a large brood—unbelievable in many ways and rare for any tiger reserve in India. A mother and five cubs! He could tell the approximate age from the size of the marks and was beside himself with excitement. Some time ago, this would have been the most unlikely place for the find. When still inhabited, the noise of the cattle, the shouts and cries of men, women, and children kept all the animals miles away. There was no possibility of shelter as all the grass and trees around had been destroyed by the villagers. But Lakarda was now deserted; after the shift, the grass had come up slowly and nature had taken over the deserted settlement. Animal life moved freely in and around it now. It was here that we believed Padmini gave birth to her family.

An immediate problem was keeping track of the movements of the tigers for, so far, no satisfactory method had been evolved to do this. (An experiment was conducted in neighbouring Nepal to determine the movement of a tiger by collaring the animal. A collar with a transmitter attached to it emits signals which allow one to track the animal's movement. In India, this experiment was conducted on other animals such as the nilgai, cheetal, and sambar; the first attempt with a tiger resulted in a casualty and the experiment was abandoned. Also, the major concern of Indian wildlife experts at the time was on keeping man's interference with the ecological system in the forest down to a minimum.) Fateh's only recourse was to keep track of the movements of the tigress by following her pugmarks and her kills, thereby attempting to establish her territory and pinpoint her presence in different areas.

As though aware that she was 'marked', Padmini began a game of hide-and-seek with him, complicating an already difficult situation.

Although Fateh Singh had been seeing masses of fresh pugmarks—indications of a large family of tigers—no actual sighting had been made. Somehow, Padmini's excessive caution had to be broken down and some kind of rapport developed between her and her human observers.

It was in early January 1977 that the tension was broken and Padmini first showed herself. Fateh was sitting in a hide near the village, hoping for some sign of the family which had been active in the area during the morning. It was twilight; the first stars were appearing in the sky. The crickets and the nightjars had started their chatter. An icy wind was blowing. Suddenly, the stillness of the night was shattered by the shrieking death cry of a buffalo. Immediately afterwards, a brooding silence enveloped the forest. Not a sound was heard in the dark.

Fateh moved off quickly towards the noise of the buffalo when the lights of the jeep caught Padmini head-on. Approximately nine feet in length, with a beautiful coat and in the best of health, she stared at him and snarled. Suddenly, in a flurry of movement, five young tigers ran across the road, disappearing into the bushy country around. It seemed as if the cubs had rushed into hiding on their mother's indication. Padmini watched Fateh carefully and with a measured tread, walked away, leaving his heart beating faster at this first sighting of the complete brood. The dawn brought Fateh back to the same area in the freezing cold. Early morning frost covered large stretches of the forest; his hands were numb from driving the jeep, his eyes smarting with the chill, but there she was, at the spot of the night before, sitting over her prey, a full-size lame buffalo which she had killed the previous night. Only a portion from the hind legs had been eaten. None of her cubs was in sight. Padmini watched Fateh suspiciously. This was amazing behaviour, for, during the day, tigers will normally find dense shelter to sleep in. But Padmini sat alert—she was guarding the meat. She knew that every ounce mattered and she would have to keep continuous vigil to prevent it from being scavenged by vultures, jackals, or hyenas. Because of the special situation, her whole pattern of behaviour had undergone a change: she was spending the day alert.

At about midday, when Fateh heard a jackal call from the left of a nearby tree, he realized that this was a definite sign that the cubs were moving towards their mother. The jackal alarm call warns of the presence of a predator. Sure enough, within ten minutes, two cubs appeared under the tree. Fateh was unable to photograph them because the branches obstructed his vision. The tigress suddenly lifted her head and seemed to signal to her offspring, who vanished instantly. Once again the jackal called, after which silence prevailed. The tigress relaxed. During all this, Fateh had stuck to only observing the scene.

Now, keeping a certain distance, he climbed up a tree and positioned himself on a branch to keep watch and to photograph. On the first click of the camera, Padmini made a threatening charge, stopping directly under the branch where Fateh sat. For a brief moment, the thought of man and tiger confronting each other on the same branch crossed Fateh's mind. But tigers very rarely climb trees, unlike other members of the cat family. Secure in this knowledge, Fateh clicked on. Padmini charged again but half-heartedly. Convinced that the man on the tree meant no harm and confident of her own prowess, she seemed to be ignoring him. She snoozed, dozed, yawned, rolled over, nibbled at the meat. The suspicion had worn off. It was as though she had started accepting his presence and was behaving naturally. For five days, from early morning to late evening, Fateh sat watching her, but all through, she kept guard with no sign of her cubs, who obviously only came at night after he had left. The carcass of the buffalo slowly diminished and on the last day, hardly anything was left, but she still sat guard. All her actions conformed to the needs of her cubs. Not an ounce of flesh was to be scavenged or wasted as long as her cubs could continue feeding on it undisturbed.

This is when we came into the picture, to add to the mounting excitement and tension. Were Padmini's young ones determined to remain invisible to us or were our efforts going to prove successful?

During the months of January and February, we saw Padmini often. She was a picture of confidence and less and less bothered by our presence so long as we maintained a certain distance. The cubs largely kept out of sight but we were fortunate enough to get fleeting glimpses of them as they rushed by. But noticeably longer stretches of observation were possible each successive time as the cubs seemed to be growing more secure in our presence.

We were now able to distinguish between the sexes and found that Padmini had three male and two female cubs. But the real question was, could Padmini manage to hunt and kill for herself as well as provide for five growing tigers, and for how long? It was a mammoth task under any circumstances. An approximate idea of the total consumption of meat would be an excellent indication of the problems facing this tiger family: Padmini had to ensure an average-to-minimum consumption of 65 to 80 kilograms of meat every few days.

The young ones were of slightly different sizes. There was one dominant male cub, tougher and fitter than his brothers and sisters. He seemed more venturesome, confident, and courageous, especially in our presence; we decided to name the male cubs, Akbar, Hamir, and Babar.

The female cubs were more fragile: smaller than Akbar and a shade smaller than Babar and Hamir; they seemed definitely more delicate and feminine. There was a slight difference even between the two of them. The smallest, whom we called Begum, was not in the best of health and gave us some worry. During our first few glimpses, she was always lagging behind the rest of the family. Poor little Begum—she was part of a very natural phenomenon in the wild where the youngest in a family is totally dominated by her brothers and sisters. It was obvious that she was getting the smallest share of the meat after a kill and that she was the shyest, eating last of all. It was a sad situation and we were worried about her chances of survival. The other female, whom we called Laxmi, was in much better condition but always one step behind her brothers.

Now that the entire family had been identified, the complex task of assimilating and analysing the different behaviour patterns of each member began. Normally, much confusion could arise in studying such a large family and distinguishing one from the other. What is important to note is that Padmini, Akbar, Babar, Hamir, Laxmi, and Begum all had different characteristics, facial expressions, and, most important of all, different markings. Tigers can be distinguished by the markings on their foreheads and around the sides of their faces. These stripes are a sure method of recognition. The stripes on the body also vary considerably and are also essential to distinguish between tigers.

Our worst suspicions regarding little Begum were confirmed during the last week of February. In the evening, we had spotted Padmini and decided to camp out on an incline in the hope of observing the family. This was an important area for water and we felt the tigers might come to drink before their siesta during the day. It was a beautiful spot with patches of tall grass interspersed with shrubs, not thick enough to obstruct our vision. Right below us was a dry river bed next to which there was a waterhole. The family had been extremely active here; it was very close to Lakarda village where Padmini had first been sighted.

We woke up with the dawn. The birds had started their chatter, the morning was cold and crisp. We crept along the ground to the edge of the incline and looked below. And there they were: Padmini walking through the grass even before the first rays of the sun were out; behind her were Akbar, followed by Babar and Hamir and then Laxmi—but not a sign of little Begum. Had she got lost somewhere, or was it possible that in the last week she had been unable to cope with the pressure of living and had given up and let nature take its course? We kept putting the thought out of our minds as we watched Padmini and her four young ones disappear into the forest. There was still a faint hope that Begum had strayed and might join them later. In any case, we decided that Begum's fate was something we needed to confirm. Accordingly, by evening, we tied up a buffalo near Lakarda; if the family killed it, it would enable us to study them closely. The time was 5 p.m. When we returned around 11 p.m., the buffalo was dead and partly eaten. On hearing the sound of the jeep, the family had moved away to a more secure position in the grass.

Using a powerful searchlight, we identified Padmini sitting beside her female cub, Laxmi. Nearby, with a slightly snarly expression on his face, sat dominant Akbar. A little behind were Babar and Hamir. Of little Begum there was no sign. What we feared had obviously happened. Begum was no more; nature had eased her out. She had been the littlest in the family and her health was affected by her position in the family hierarchy. She had not been able to get enough food and had probably just wasted away.

3

ABOUT TIGERS

The binomial nomenclature of the tiger, the largest of the big cats, is *Panthera tigris*. The lion, leopard, and jaguar also belong to the *Panthera* genus—the name given to big cats that have a special roar, made possible by the vibration of the thickened vocal folds just below the vocal cords in the larynx. *Tigris* is the species name that differentiates the tiger from other members of the genus: *Panthera leo* (lion), *Panthera pardus* (leopard), and *Panthera onca* (jaguar). *Tigris* derives from the Armenian (Persian) word for 'arrow' after which the straight and swiftly flowing river was named as well.

The origins of the tiger trace back to some 50 million years, 15 million years after the mass extinction of dinosaurs, and flying and swimming reptiles—an extinction that paved the way for mammals. The tiger's earliest ancestors were miacids—tree-climbing creatures that bore a resemblance to today's pine martens.

The direct ancestors of today's big cats were the Pseudaelurus, which lived about 20 million years ago. Molecular techniques used to compare the genetic similarities among the modern-day members of the *Panthera* genus have determined that it was the tiger that first diverged from the common *Panthera* ancestor;

the lion, leopard, and jaguar evolved much later and have a stronger genetic resemblance to one another than with the tiger.

The period popularly termed the ice age, which occurred between 2.6 million and 12,000 years ago, was actually a series of ninety or more cold cycles intermixed with warmer periods. About 2 million years ago, our ancestor, *Homo habilis*, began to evolve into *Homo erectus* and eventually began moving out of Africa. The modern *Homo sapiens* did not exist until about 40,000 years ago and many believe that they evolved from archaic humans nearly 200,000 years ago in Africa. The existence of tigers at this time cannot be definitely proved by the distribution of tiger fossils, which provide most of the evidence scientists and researchers have used to piece together our understanding of the tiger. The reason for this is that tigers and lions look very similar when stripped of their stripes and manes, and incomplete, badly weathered skeletons have made the job of identification exceedingly difficult. Moreover, tigers tend to live in dense forest, with lots of moisture, heat, and mud—conditions which don't help fossil formation.

The earliest tiger fossils are 1 to 2 million years old and have been found in China, Java, and Sumatra. Those in Russia have been traced back to 700,000 years, and those in India are only 10,000 years old. Though a few fossils have been found in Beringia, the strip of land that connected Asia to North America during the ice ages, there is no evidence that tigers entered North America, although recent fossil evidence suggests that they existed in Borneo as recently as a few hundred years ago.

From the existing, scant fossil evidence, scientists have formed two alternative theories. The most accepted version is the Asian theory. It asserts that more than 2 million years ago, when early man had yet to venture out of Africa, tigers separated from their big cat cousins in East Asia, with the South China form being the original template. They split up in two directions. One group travelled north to Russia while the second spread south-east to the Indonesian islands and south-west to India. The second theory debates the notion that there was a single point of origin in China, as natural selection acting on an isolated but geographically widespread population could also result in its simultaneous evolution elsewhere.

The last major ice age ended approximately 12,000 years ago. During that time, people and animals had been able to cross from continental Europe to Britain by foot. Now, the ice at the poles melted, and the North Sea and Irish Sea and the English Channel became too deep to cross. The land became warmer and trees grew, creating forests across Britain. European lions, which had been common for 900,000 years, became extinct. The Sahara received more rain and became habitable. In North America, sabre-toothed cats and the American lion were becoming extinct. It is at this time, as fossils discovered at the Kurnool cave deposits in Andhra Pradesh tell us, that the tiger first entered India.

Their relationship with humans can be traced back 5,000 years, as the discovery of rock paintings from that period in Indian cave sites show. These paintings depict men and various animals, including the tiger, either resting or running, and many of the hunting scenes feature tigers. The peoples of the Indus Valley civilization were the first to use the tiger as an important symbol in their cultures. Tiger engravings on seals have been found. They are believed to have marked the ownership of property and were also worn as amulets.

Whatever scant fossil evidence has been found of this period, suggests that the tiger population maintained a wide distribution and equilibrium, with humans being far less numerous and lethal than they are now.

More than a thousand years ago, the Roman empire was at its peak. The use of Caspian tigers and Indian tigers in their games and in massacres in their amphitheatres introduced the first significant threat to the tiger's existence. The tiger population began to go into decline more than a century ago, when the proliferation of firearms and cars facilitated hunting for sport and medicinal purposes. People also began hunting the tiger's prey and encroaching upon its natural habitats, converting them to agricultural lands. In the fifty years between 1875 and 1925, 80,000 tigers were killed in India alone and an equal number were probably injured and died later of their wounds.

Today, there are an estimated 3,000 to 3,500 tigers in the wild. They span fourteen countries, from the snowy lands of eastern Russia to the sweltering jungles of Sumatra. Tigers live in temperatures that range from -33 °C (-27.4 °F) in the northern extreme of their range to 50 °C (122 °F) in the southern part, and at altitudes that range from sea level to 3,000 metres (nearly 10,000 feet). Vegetation also varies greatly. Tigers are incredibly versatile animals, requiring only dense vegetative cover, large ungulate prey, and water to survive. Tigers living in the north are generally larger and paler, with thick, shaggy coats, while those in the south, which live in jungle and heat, are smaller, darker, and have shorter fur.

Tigers were originally divided into eight subspecies, often with country-specific names, but recent research, led by Andrew Kitchener, principal curator of vertebrates at National Museums Scotland, has reduced the number of tiger subspecies. Today, the world's current population of tigers represents five of the original eight subspecies: the Amur (*Panthera tigris altaica*), the Bengal (*Panthera tigris tigris*), the Indo-Chinese (*Panthera tigris corbetti*), the South China (*Panthera tigris amoyensis*), and the Sumatran (*Panthera tigris sumatrae*). The first four are classified as the Asian tiger (*Panthera tigris tigris*), the last as the Sunda Islands tiger. At least three of the original eight subspecies are now extinct—the Caspian tiger, the Javan tiger, and the Balinese tiger. South China tigers have not been seen in the wild for several decades, and though footprints and kills have been found, it is generally believed that they are either extinct, or close to extinction.

◆

The tiger, considered one of the world's most dangerous predators, is situated firmly at the top of the food chain. In order to survive, it needs to consume at least one deer-sized animal each week, and its anatomy has evolved to make it a perfect hunter.

The tiger's skeleton facilitates both speed and strength. Their long hindlegs enable them to leap forward 10 metres (32.5 feet) while their small collarbone increases the length of their stride. Their forelegs, the muscles of which are supported by solid forelimb bones, give tigers incredible power, and the closely bound ligaments in their feet help them survive the impact of landing, which is crucial to their ability to sprint. Tigers also have a short, rounded skull which makes their jaws more powerful. Their jaws cannot move from side to side, which adds strength to their bite, and their septum is made of bone, unlike that of humans and many other animals whose septum comprises only a membrane; this increases the strength of their skull. Tigers have thirty teeth, the largest canines of all the big cats, measuring 5 to 7.5 centimetres long. These canines consist of nerves that are extremely sensitive to pressure, which increases the accuracy of their bite, enabling them to locate and sever the spinal cord. The tiger's tongue is rough and covered with many minuscule, sharp objects known as papillae, which helps it to remove feathers, fur, and lick meat clean off the bone.

Claws play a significant role in the tiger's hunting abilities. A tiger's claws can be as long as 10 centimetres (4 inches), and they help the tiger to hold its prey down before the deadly bite. Tigers have four claws on each paw, as well as a dewclaw on the front ones which aid it in gripping prey and climbing. Claws are kept retracted when not in use—tigers walk on their toes, which have big, soft pads to help them move without any noise.

The tiger's whiskers, too, help its sense of touch. The whiskers on its face are embedded in capsules of blood. When they brush against something, the root of the whisker moves, amplifying the movement, causing the nerves to send a signal to the brain.

The tiger's tail, often more than a metre long, also aids it in hunting—it gathers force when swung, helping the animal to balance if it has to make a sudden turn during a chase. It also helps in communication: a tiger waves a raised tail upon meeting an acquaintance, but holds it low with an occasional twitch, or swings it violently if it is feeling aggressive.

Tigers have short, relatively uncomplicated guts, since meat can be converted to protein more easily than grass. They also have small, light abdomens which help in the acceleration of their speed. Renowned mammalogist and conservationist George B. Schaller made a study of the scat of emaciated tigers, and discovered the presence of grass and tapeworms, concluding that tigers sometimes eat grass in order to rid their intestines of parasites. Their digestive system is remarkable—other studies have shown that their stomachs can cope with porcupine quills and bear claws.

The tiger's magnificent stripes provide it with excellent camouflage. It has been suggested that the reason white tigers are so rare in the wild is because they lose the ability to conceal themselves and thus seldom survive to birth cubs. The tiger's fur traps air, insulating its body to a steady temperature of 37 °C (99 °F). Longer fur helps heat retention, which is why tigers in colder climates have longer fur than those that live in the hotter southern regions. Tigers shed their fur twice a year, their summer coat being shorter than their winter coat. They use their tongue to groom themselves. The tongue is also important in healing injuries as licking wounds coats them with antiseptic saliva. The colour of a tiger's coat ranges from pale yellow, such as is seen on tigers in cold, northern climates, to the deep orange more commonly found in the south. Since the colour range within a subspecies varies widely, it is not regarded as a definitive species characteristic.

Like all cats, tigers have excellent sight in the dark. Their eyes have sensitive cells that absorb light. The retina contains two different kinds of cells: rods and cones. Rods respond to low levels of light and cones, which are used in colour vision, respond to high levels. Tigers have more rods than cones, and as a result, they have superior night vision, which is useful for hunting, at the expense of colour vision. A reflective retinal layer known as the tapetum lucidum causes their eyes to glow in the dark and also facilitates night vision. Tigers have binocular vision—their eyes create a sort of 3D image—which is crucial to their ability in calculating their distance from their prey and striking with accuracy. A 'visual streak' close to the centre of the eye makes them extremely sensitive to movement, much more than humans.

Tigers, like other carnivores, have a small pouch on the roof of their mouth called the Jacobson's organ which allows them to analyse and identify scent. Although a sense of smell is not crucial to hunting, it is extremely important for communication. Adult tigers are solitary animals and their sense of smell helps them to make sense of what is going on in their surroundings. For instance, they use scent to mark their territory or to find a mate at the appropriate time.

The tiger's most highly developed sense is its ability to hear. Tigers have large ear flaps or pinnae that help them to catch various kinds of sounds, as well as to locate the precise origin of these sounds. Sensitive to both high-frequency and low-frequency sound waves, their hearing range is far more extensive than that of humans. Like elephants and whales, they often communicate by infrasound which can travel over long distances and thick forest cover because of its ability to pass straight through solid objects such as trees and mountains. All these aspects of the tiger's anatomy come together harmoniously and contribute towards making it a superb hunter.

4

GENGHIS, THE MASTER HUNTER

Nearly a decade after I first got there, during 1983–84, Ranthambhore witnessed an extraordinary and quite exceptional form of tiger predation when one particular resident male developed a technique for attacking and killing his prey in the water, concentrating his activities around the three lakes named Padam Talao, Rajbagh Talao, and Malik Talao. Nowhere in the literature of the past were we able to find any other account of a tiger behaving in this way. As a strategist, he was unmatched—an innovator. We called him Genghis.

By early March 1984, Genghis was a regular feature at the lakes. On one occasion, as he lay camouflaged in tall grass, a group of wild boar unsuspectingly approached him. In a flash, he leapt and pounced on a piglet and swatted another with his paws. Carrying them one at a time, he entered the grass to eat. We found him the next morning, protecting the scraps of the leftover meat from his feast. He was exceedingly aggressive then and charged at our jeep once, roaring in anger. By 11 a.m., after consuming the leftovers, he moved to Rajbagh where he went to sleep in the grass. A couple of hours later, four sambar came around the edge of the lake where he was. As they approached him, he charged out of the grass, giving chase but unsuccessfully. He went back into the grass where he remained until sunset.

Late one morning, a few days later, we found Genghis walking towards Malik Talao where he disappeared into the tall grass. At 11.30 a.m., a group of four adult sambar approached the lake shore. Immediately, Genghis popped his head out of the grass and started moving diagonally through it in the direction of the deer. Just as he reached the edge of the cover, a peahen burst into flight nearby. Startled by the sound, one of the sambar turned—and spotted the tiger. As the deer started to stamp and bellow an alarm call, Genghis charged, but the bird had ruined his attack. The range was too great, and as the sambar leapt away, calling frantically, he broke off the charge and, with an expression of annoyance, padded slowly back into the cover of the grass thicket.

Despite the summer heat, the lake was strangely quiet for much of the afternoon. A small herd of cheetal grazed on the far side of the lake; a few sambar entered the shallows, grazed a while, and then drifted away, but there was little activity in our immediate vicinity. A golden oriole chirped away on a nearby tree and a pair of paradise flycatchers settled at the edge of the lake to drink. I had almost given up hope of the sambar returning.

Just after 5 p.m., two groups of sambar appeared—approaching from opposite ends of the lake and wading steadily towards the centre, right opposite our observation point. A slight movement stirred the tall grass at the far side of the lake where we knew Genghis lay hidden. A face appeared. He had moved right to the edge of the thicket and was peering out, studying the sambar with intense concentration. For several minutes, he stood there, motionless, like a statue.

The next thirty minutes were some of the most tense and exciting moments I have ever lived through. Our sweating hands gripped our cameras and notebooks as we waited, with hearts thumping, for the tiger to make his move. With incredible patience, Genghis waited, measuring the distance separating him from the sambar grazing peacefully in the water. And then he charged. In front of our furiously clicking cameras, he crashed through the few remaining metres of long grass and plunged into the water. The lake seemed to erupt in an explosion of spray. Bounding through the water, he made for a small group of hinds and their fawns, then changed direction to concentrate his attack on one terrified fawn that had got separated from its mother in the panic. The young deer was doomed from that moment. Covering the last few metres with swift, powerful strokes, Genghis pounced, driving his victim under the surface, then reappearing seconds later with the fawn's neck clenched in a killer grip.

We watched in amazement. Never before had we seen a tiger even attempt to launch an attack in the waters of the lake, nor was it something we had ever come across in old accounts. Was this just an aberration, or were we seeing something new?

We left the lake at dusk in a state of elation. We had witnessed an astonishing feat, a successful hunt in water. Even better, we had captured the entire attack on film. Genghis was now making effective use of the area of the lakes and utilizing it fully as a hunting ground. He had somehow managed to use the water to his own advantage, unlike the surprised sambar which had lost vital seconds watching the tiger bounding after it through the water. The camouflage of the tall grass was perfect.

And this was not just an unusual day. Genghis spent twenty-four days between the second week of March and the second week of April using the same strategy in Malik Talao. He killed six young sambar. This strategy was obviously effective on the younger animals who seemed to lose precious time in their confusion. But the summer heat was increasing and the water level in Malik Talao was dropping rapidly. By early April, there was a wide gap between the grass and the water and Genghis's success rate was diminishing. He now had to cover quite a distance on dry land before hitting the water, and the sambar had more time in which to make their escape. In the second week of April, we witnessed one of the last successful kills that Genghis made in Malik Talao.

In response to the changing situation, Genghis switched his activities to Padam Talao, still using his new strategy of attacking in the water. Padam Talao was much larger than Malik Talao, and on most of its shoreline, there was still the cover of tall grass thickets. Naturally, we followed, and soon discovered that the best vantage point from which to observe the attacks was Jogi Mahal itself, which is located on the edge of the lake. Besides charging into the water to kill, Genghis also tried two other strategies. In the first, he would see a group of sambar from the grass and then come right up to the edge of the water, out in the open, to watch them, causing the sambar to bolt in alarm. As this lake is large, it is not possible for the sambar to cross from one side to the other with ease. Instead, they invariably bolted towards the corners, and Genghis would attempt to cut off these exits and make his kill as the deer fled from the lake. To do this, he sometimes had to run nearly 150 metres, which, at full pelt, is an amazing feat and one that invited comparison with the technique of the cheetah. His other strategy was to swim out into the lake, pursuing groups of sambar with powerful strokes and causing much confusion. If, in this process, a single animal got separated, Genghis would overpower it with ease. He seemed to patrol all sides of the lake, constantly watching the entry and exit points. Sometimes, in the terrible heat of the afternoon, he would spot a group of sambar in one corner and then stalk them for some 200 metres before charging. If there was a jeep on the road watching the scene, he would stalk around the jeep, moving with it and using it as cover for his final ambush. But Genghis's hunting forays into the water were not without problems. Padam Talao had some sixty marsh crocodiles and as Genghis was killing in the water, he came into aggressive conflict with the larger ones. On one such occasion, he was found sitting at the edge of the lake, looking carefully at a spot in the water. He sat for several hours, watching as crocodiles splashed and nibbled around what must have been the carcass of a sambar. Twice he swam back and attacked the spot where he thought there was a carcass, but in vain. On the third occasion, he went back into the water and in great fury, smashed at the water with his forepaws. Dipping his head down, he quickly grabbed the carcass and made for shore. He had to swim at least 45 metres and still managed to keep a grip on the carcass, which was of an adult sambar hind. While swimming, he wrapped a paw around the sambar's neck and used the other paw to stroke the water. Once, for a moment, he disappeared under the water with the carcass but quickly surfaced again and powerfully stroked his way to dry land. An amazing feat—a tiger swimming to shore with an animal weighing at least 200 kilograms.

With his long bursts of speed, Genghis used the water to his advantage. Unlike Genghis, most other tigers take up a position near water or long grass and try to remain undetected until prey comes along. It is a game of patience and success depends on the wisdom and experience of the tiger. Usually, one in ten attacks is successful.

Genghis was the monarch of all he surveyed and never tolerated any competition. In my years of watching tigers, I have never encountered one like him. It was like watching a tactical planner who had evolved an extraordinary way of hunting after assessing the lakes and all their nuances. He passed on this technique of predation to the resident tigress Noon.

5

NOON, THE TIGRESS
I FELL IN LOVE WITH

The area of the lakes in Ranthambhore is where Fateh and I spent the best days of our lives. It is where his ashes have been sprinkled and where mine will go. This was where I spent much of the 1980s, observing and photographing Noon, a tigress from Padmini's second litter. Noon engaged me like no other tiger had done. I lived then in Jogi Mahal, which was the heart of Noon's area, and in minutes I could rush off to find her.

Towards the end of May in the mid-1980s, I received a cable from Fateh that read, 'Come immediately. Noon has given birth to two cubs.' I was ecstatic. Noon was then five years old. I was in Ranthambhore by early June and Fateh told me how he had discovered Noon's very first litter a few days earlier. He had been in the middle of breakfast at Jogi Mahal when one of the people who worked for him, Badhyaya, came running to tell him that road workers some 500 metres away had stumbled onto two tiny, cat-like creatures in thick bush. Fateh had never seen newly born cubs—were they tiger or leopard?

Camera in hand, he rushed off on foot with Badhyaya. It was dangerous but he could not take the jeep into the ravine. A tigress with small cubs will charge as aggression is a way to protect and defend them. Fateh had seen

Noon mating twice, so this bush required investigation. The tension mounted as they walked into the dense ravine. The fort of Ranthambhore loomed overhead. The road workers who had discovered the cubs stood by in a nervous cluster and Fateh told them to go home. Fateh and Badhyaya walked towards the thick bush in which the cubs had been found.

Fateh was not easily frightened by anything but he confessed to me that this was the most nerve-racking moment of his life—not knowing what would come charging out at him. He assumed the mother was away. Paradise flycatchers flew overhead. A couple of golden orioles flitted around a mango tree. A small stream flowed through the thickly forested ravine. The setting was wild and picturesque. The thick bush had a few plants around it and was dark inside. Gradually, Fateh's and Badhyaya's eyes adjusted to the dark. Fateh peered in. A slight movement caught his eye as a tiny, snarling, striped ball revealed itself. Tiger cubs. Fateh quickly took a few photographs of what appeared to be two-week-old cubs whose eyes were open. In the distance, peacocks started alarm-calling. Fateh's heart thudded. Noon could be returning. He still had to confirm the tigress's identity, so he quickly told Badhyaya to close the tracks to all humans and then crawled up a ledge to a vantage point above the ravine. Two hours later, he saw Noon approach the bush. This is what we had all been hoping for. She had a perfect den but it was too close to the road on which a continuous stream of pilgrims made their way up to the Ganesh temple each day.

That night, Fateh was fast asleep on the terrace under the open sky. In the heat of the summer, sleeping on the terrace is the only way to remain cool. At 4.45 a.m., the peace and stillness of the night were suddenly shattered by the alarm calls of sambar and the barking of a troop of langurs. Fateh, jolted from sleep, tumbled out of bed and looked down. A predator was on the move. The first rays of morning light crept across the horizon. On the vehicle track below, Noon was striding along, carrying one of her cubs in her mouth. She crossed some ruins and clambered over an ancient wall disappearing into one of the most inaccessible areas below the ramparts of the fort. She was changing dens and soon returned and carried her second cub to the new spot. Fateh watched from the terrace. Noon had now found one of the safest spots in her range to den her cubs. This was a great relief for Fateh as she was now away from all human disturbance. For me, it was the beginning of two splendid years of watching mother and cubs.

Birthing amongst tigers is no easy process. After a

gestation period of 93 to 110 days, the tigress chooses a safe spot to deliver her cubs. Cubs can be born within one hour but sometimes the birth can take as long as twenty-four hours, during which time the tigress gets some nourishment from eating the placenta and embryonic sac. The cubs are born blind and helpless, weighing between 0.79 to 1.5 kilograms. It takes anywhere from three to fourteen days for their eyes to open, though full vision is not acquired until some weeks later. There may be six or seven cubs in a litter, though in Ranthambhore, the average is three. The ratio of sexes at birth is one to one.

Early one morning on the day I was to leave on that visit to see Noon and her cubs, a huge storm came crashing through the park—thunder, lightning, and torrents of rain. Visibility was down to less than a metre. The monsoon was approaching. Within an hour, the ferocious storm cleared up, leaving in its wake a blue sky and the early-morning sun. The forest was washed clean. The quality of light was special. The fragrance in the air was magical. The leaves dripped with water and torrents of water cascaded down the hillside, and waterfalls sprouted from the steep cliff faces and the edges of the fort. As we turned a bend in the road, Noon crossed our path. One season had ended and another was about to start.

In 1986, Prime Minister Rajiv Gandhi visited Ranthambhore with his family. News of Fateh's success with the tigers had reached his ears. Hosting the then-prime minister and his family was one of Fateh's greatest delights. And for a whole week, Noon entertained the visitors, which culminated in an attack on a sambar at the edge of Rajbagh. She raced into the shallow water, missed one deer, and killed another sambar in a flash as huge sheets of water rose into the air under the hooves of the fleeing herd. The time of her attack was just after noon and she dragged the carcass away to feed in high grass, only a few feet away from where the prime minister stood watching. He wanted to see more of her in the high grass but his security personnel were reluctant. Eventually, a bullet-proof vehicle was summoned and Fateh went into the high grass with the prime minister. They were stunned to see a big male feeding on the carcass. It was Broken Tooth. The prime minister was surprised to see Noon sitting and watching from a little distance away. Fateh told me that the prime minister remarked that just like a traditional Indian woman, the tigress had provided a meal for her mate! It was soon after this visit that tourism boomed. Another era was about to begin. Fateh was thrilled. His dream of Ranthambhore being the ultimate tiger destination on earth was about to come true because of tigers like Noon.

◆

In Noon's first year as the resident tigress of the lakes, she engaged intensely with the big male whom we had named Genghis. He mated with her at the same time that Broken Tooth mated with her. Her litter could have been fathered by either one of these big males. Genghis, the Lord of the Lakes, taught Noon how to kill in the water. She attacked crocodiles, usurped their kills, and chased sambar into the water, successfully disposing of them Genghis-style. After Genghis's departure, Noon became his alter ego, as far as killing in the water was concerned. In the first six months after Genghis left, Noon's water attacks were a little hesitant and lacked her mentor's expertise, but slowly, she mastered this art.

I remember one hot afternoon in March when Noon charged into the water from the grass, missing a sambar by inches. She then walked back into the grass and, an hour later, carefully watched another group of sambar entering the water some 100 metres away. They were after the succulent aquatic plants that grow in the lakes. In typical Genghis fashion, she stalked the sambar through the grass. She was developing her strategy through practice. She erupted from the grass and raced into the water a few feet away from the sambar but again, they escaped. I had now seen nearly twenty unsuccessful charges. Later the same evening, she charged at yet another group of sambar in the far corner of the lake, this time chasing her victim across the shore to cut off its exit. But in vain.

At the critical moment of impact, she would pause, but she was learning from her mistakes. One day, I watched her racing into the water after a group of sambar and in the confusion, most of the deer fled but two helpless fawns remained and in panic, moved into deeper water. Noon struck with lightning speed and killed one of them. I knew then that she would be a real proponent of the Genghis technique. As spring and summer arrived, her forays into the water became more regular, and in a five-week period between March and April 1985, Noon killed six sambar fawns in the water. The sambars' addiction to the succulent water plants continued, with complete disregard for the high level of predation they faced.

One of Noon's typical attacks to scavenge off the crocodiles revealed her mastery over this predator. Three large crocodiles had attacked a medium-sized sambar hind in the waters of Rajbagh. The depth of the water in which they struggled with the deer was not more than 1.5 metres. One crocodile made desperate efforts to yank off a hind leg, while another tried to grab the neck, amidst much turning and twisting of their bodies for leverage. The sambar was frozen, locked in by the jaws of crocodiles (many more had arrived now) on all sides. Other sambar on the edges were calling out in alarm. After a few ear-splitting shrieks, the captive sambar sank underwater and was hidden from view by a swirling mass of crocodiles. With much splashing and snapping, the crocodiles tried to tear the carcass apart. It was a slow and noisy process. The reptiles didn't seem to have much success in feeding off the dead sambar.

Suddenly, Noon and her sub-adult cubs appeared, attracted by all the noise. Tigers will immediately respond to any sound of an animal being attacked either by other tigers, leopards, or crocodiles. The cubs sat on their haunches as Noon circled the shore, moving towards the crocodiles. She watched them for a few minutes and then slowly entered the shallow water. She gingerly picked her way towards the action some 10 metres away. She paused 4 metres away and then, with a burst of speed, arrived at the carcass. She was smashing the water with her paws all the while and this forced the crocodiles to retreat. Twenty crocodiles glided away hastily. Grabbing the neck of the sambar, she pulled it through the water to her waiting cubs. A large, interfering crocodile got slapped. After a Herculean effort, she reached the shore where her cubs raced towards her. They nuzzled her and pawed the carcass but she still had to drag it 50 metres to the cover of high grass. While she was doing this, her male cub pulled at her tail as if to say, 'I want to help.' Noon's male cub was slowly turning into a lake expert, following in his mother's footsteps. The female cub was reticent.

Young cubs learn about hunting from the age of three to four months and stalk anything that moves— insects, butterflies, frogs, partridges, and even quails. In peacock-infested forests, they chase and eat peacocks, plucking off their feathers and devouring their meat. I watched Noon and her sub-adults race after a single peafowl and swipe it with their huge paws before its clumsy take-off. Noon would also devour porcupines. She was never injured by a quill but I have seen other tigers embedded with quills which they try desperately to pluck out. It is astonishing how they enjoy feeding on an animal that is so tough to kill. Another animal that is occasionally killed is the ratel or honey badger, which sometimes arrives at carcasses to scavenge.

Occasionally, when she was hunting, Noon would

look skywards and follow the direction vultures took, especially when they were flying low and swooping to the ground. I once watched her following low-flying vultures at a fast trot from one lake to another until she found the carcass of a young sambar. At the time, Ranthambhore was full of white-backed vultures. Sadly, today, there are hardly any left. A chemical injected to treat livestock proved harmful when ingested by vultures scavenging on carcasses, resulting in their population being wiped out. India lost a cleaning service provided by nature. Noon lost her food finders. In the absence of vultures, crows are good indicators of kills and the chatter of treepies can also lead to a carcass. But when a tiger turns up, vultures and crows become the object of the master scavenger's wrath.

At the end of 1987, Noon had her second litter. In the first months after they were born, the cubs were very curious and playful. They centred their activities in the vicinity of Jogi Mahal, where they were born. One day, we followed them into one of their densest day shelters and found the male cub perched high up in a tree. Up to the age of fifteen months, the cubs enjoy climbing and sitting on trees. They are light enough, so the branches don't break. Noon sat below and watched as the female cub tried unsuccessfully to clamber up to her brother who kept smacking her down. Soon, the cubs abandoned their game and snuggled up to their mother. As she licked both of them, they rubbed cheeks and flanks with her. One of the cubs jumped over her and caught her tail. She then rolled over on her back as one of the cubs stretched across her belly. The cubs chased each other around, leaping at each other, while standing up on their hind legs. Wrestling and gentle sparring strengthen the family bond, and this use of their limbs is vital to develop their strength.

In late January 1988, we set off in search of Noon and her cubs on a bitingly cold morning. A langur was barking in alarm at the edge of Rajbagh and we went to investigate. The sun was rising over the hill, and as we switched off the engine, we were greeted by a cacophony of sambar, chital, and langur alarm calls. At one corner of the lake, Noon was walking along nonchalantly with a chital fawn swinging from her mouth. A few peahens took flight. She headed for a bank of high grass. Suddenly, two peacocks flew out of the grass, followed by two racing cubs. They rushed to Noon and the male cub grabbed the fawn and darted back into the clump of grass. Noon licked the female cub and they both reclined at the edge of the grass. They waited patiently for the more aggressive male to have his fill. The male polished off the best parts but was soon pushed away by Noon amidst much growling. She picked up the remnants and her male cub moved away. The female cub joined her mother and they chewed on the bits and pieces that were left. After an hour, mother and cubs left the grass and walked around the shore towards Padam Talao. The cubs were in a great mood and jumped and chased each other as they walked. One charged into Noon and she snarled in annoyance. They now reached the edge of the lake; the cubs went along the side of the lake and Noon followed the jeep path. In between, there were forest and deer. Suddenly, two sambar alarms blasted out from the lake as the cubs flushed the deer. Noon was now completely alert and darted rapidly on to the track realizing that the sambar were between her and her cubs. There was a thud of hooves as Noon settled down on her belly, completely still, at a point where the animal track joined the road. A large rock hid her. She had judged the exit perfectly and it looked as if her cubs were helping. Suddenly, she leapt up and I saw the flash of a sambar head going down. A grunt and a dying croak were all we heard as she clutched the throat of a sambar hind. It was a perfect grip and the sambar's legs twitched in vain. The cubs approached the carcass but were frightened by the thrashing leg movements of the sambar. In minutes, the sambar was dead. The male cub came in and rested his paw on the sambar's shoulder. I was astounded—two kills in less than two hours. The female cub sniffed at the carcass and soon, Noon dragged it into the thicket. The cubs had watched the killing and helped to flush out the sambar. They would now feast for a few days. We had seen the first joint forays made by the mother and cubs—these would help the cubs develop and fine-tune their hunting skills.

By the age of sixteen months, the cubs had grown large. They wandered around their mother's range, keeping in touch with her through scent and sound. Noon tried her best to encourage their independence. I remember, late one evening, around Malik Talao, a burst of alarm calls indicated the presence of Noon in a clump of grass. As we approached, she charged and killed a chital fawn. As she walked along, carrying the dead fawn, her cubs darted towards her. The male attempted to snatch away the fawn. The cubs were now large enough to battle for the fawn; the female gripped one end of it and for a while, both cubs remained motionless, holding onto either end of the fawn. Then began a frantic tug of war and the fawn was rocked from side to side. This time around, Noon reclined to one side as her cubs fought over the right to eat first. Several shattering growls later, the male cub had won the bout. It is at this age that the cubs are forced to fend for themselves and make their first attempts at stalking and hunting peafowl, monkeys, and fawns. It is a critical period where their ability to survive is tested. Noon's absences from around her growing cubs became longer.

Noon had to be very careful about other male tigers who could intrude into her territory. For example, Broken Tooth, whom she later mated with, encountered her over one of her kills. She boxed him on the nose to defend herself. She lost the bout but fortunately, didn't suffer much damage. Such fights can be vicious and I know of at least one case in which a tigress killed a tiger in order to protect her cubs. The male cub faces the biggest threat from transient male tigers.

Our final observation of Noon's second litter was in May 1989. Late one afternoon, we were watching large herds of chital congregating on the shores of Rajbagh Lake where the waters were fast receding. It was hot and in a month monsoon clouds would fill the sky. As we looked on, the male cub moved out of a patch of grass watched by hundreds of chital, all alarm-calling in panic. But he was in no mood to hunt. Looking well fed, he walked leisurely to the water and settled in it to cool off and quench his thirst. The deer alarms petered out. Half an hour later, Noon appeared on the far side and did much the same thing and then 30 metres away, the female cub came out to cool off. The cubs were now nearly their mother's size. The three tigers soaked in the water. The deer watched but continued grazing. The sun was setting. It was my last day in Ranthambhore on that visit. The saga of this family group was nearly over.

Noon survived the 1980s and my last sighting of her was in the summer of 1990. I will never forget that encounter. She walked slowly to the edge of Rajbagh Lake. She looked older. Tigers change colour as they age, especially around the face, where the hair grows paler. The monsoon would soon crash down and I was not sure if I would see her again. The sun was setting and its rays glanced off her back, enveloping her in a golden light.

This time, too, as always, she was a tigress who filled up my senses. I am reminded here of a comment Fateh had teased me with—that I had fallen in love with this tigress. I know that whenever I arrived in her presence, there was a quick look of recognition and then, most of the time, it was just her and me. Many scientist friends warned me to keep detached and not humanize tigers, but in truth, I was delighted with my emotional engagement with Noon. It deepened my understanding of the mysterious world of tigers.

6

THE SEX LIFE OF TIGERS

The entire 1980s were the years that Broken Tooth—or Kublai, as Fateh preferred to call him—ruled the territory that I traversed. He patrolled the Kachida Valley and the edge of Lakarda where the Bakaula male reigned. He made the rounds of the lakes and the Nalghati Valley, traversing more than 100 square kilometres. In his prime, he expanded his domain considerably but his field of influence decreased towards the end of the 1980s.

I first photographed him one night when he was eighteen months old, just when he was about to separate from his family. For male tigers, this is the beginning of a challenging period. By twenty to twenty-two months, they lose all contact with the mother and move to the fringes of an area to hunt, eat, and develop in size, strength, and ability. It takes a year and sometimes even two years for them to mature to match the powers of the resident male. Sometimes, they can be pushed out of the park. A few have been known to move from Ranthambhore, all the way to Madhya Pradesh. Tigers are very difficult to see or find during this period after dispersal from the family unit. By paying attention to the scent marks of other tigers, they stay away from any direct confrontation. If they encounter a big male, the conflict is usually soon resolved. I once witnessed such an encounter between two males late at night. One was slightly larger than the other. They rushed at each other with the most blood-curdling roars. It was chilling to watch. Nose to nose, they snarled ferociously at each other, but in seconds, the younger male dropped to the ground and rolled over on his back in a gesture of submission. The conflict was over and the resident male silently walked away. Serious problems arise when males of equal strength compete with each other and neither is ready to submit. In some of these encounters, a tiger can be killed and eaten by the victor. I have never encountered such an event but there are many records of fatal encounters from across India. There are times when a tigress can confront large transient males. As I've said in the last chapter, I know of a case where a tigress confronted and killed a big male to protect her cubs. She even opened the carcass of the male and ate a bit of the rump. Roaring loudly, she then took her cubs away.

I do not know what tortuous experiences Broken Tooth went through between the age of two and four years but he survived and took over a prime bit of tiger turf. He was a gentle male who was rarely aggressive in my presence. He kept his distance from human observers, unlike Genghis, and if you got too close, he would tend to move off. He was squat-bodied and when full of food, the folds of his belly nearly scraped the ground as he walked. He was much paler then Genghis and less adventurous. A few years after I saw him, he broke half a tooth probably while killing a sambar and assumed his name. Earlier, we had referred to him as the big male of the lakes.

Big males like Broken Tooth enjoy walking. I remember a day in the early 1980s when I saw Broken Tooth in the middle of the road as I entered the gate at Jogi Mahal. It was 7 a.m. and I followed him as he skirted Padam Talao. When the resident male arrives in an area, he usually leaves territorial signals by marking all the trees. That morning, Broken Tooth was in a marking mood and he must have spray-marked three trees before he sniffed the air and hung his tongue out in a display of flehmen, the tiger's behavioural response to another tiger's scent. In this gesture the tiger curls back its upper lip exposing its front teeth and inhaling heavily. This position is held for several seconds and facilitates the transfer of pheromones and other scents into the vomero nasal or Jacobson's organ located above the roof of the mouth via a duct behind the front teeth. These chemical cues provide enormous information on the reproductive status and freshness of the presence of other tigers. The tiger scans the area and then re-marks the spot where he has identified another tiger's scent. This signal is important to attract or repel conflict.

Walking with tigers is a great delight. Especially in the early morning. As the sun rises, the golden light slides off the tiger's body. It is a magnificent spectacle. In the winter, as the tiger breathes, puffs of mist explode from his mouth. Sometimes, these walks lead him to the resident female and her cubs. He checks his harem and bonds with the cubs. Tigers can walk more than 10 kilometres in a night and Broken Tooth was no exception. As has been noted, males are territorial and as they walk, they sniff their marking trees and spray them. They can do this every 100 yards, especially after the monsoon as their scent gets washed out. If the scent is fresh, other tigers mostly change direction to avoid clashes. However, if a new male wants control of a territory, he will follow the scent until he finds the resident. A battle royal could follow but I have never witnessed this between equally powerful males. In Ranthambhore, conflicts were mainly resolved by scent-marking. Scrape marks are also left behind on the grassy verges of paths and roads. Male tigers defecate at important spots in their range.

Broken Tooth had mated with Noon but so had

Genghis. We remain unsure to this day as to who fathered that first litter of Noon's. I had watched Broken Tooth court Noon but missed the actual mating, which Fateh recorded. Fateh's diary reveals the magic of mating tigers.

For a week before their mating, Broken Tooth and Noon were always together. It was like a courtship period and there was a constant sharing of kills, which Broken Tooth ate from first. At four o'clock one afternoon, Fateh witnessed the tigers mating in the back pools of Rajbagh Lake. It was a stormy day and black clouds filled the sky. At 5 p.m., Noon emerged from the thicket and sat at the edge of the water. Soon, Broken Tooth appeared and sat a few metres away. Noon quickly got up and moved to the male, rubbing flanks, and nuzzling him seductively before sitting down in front of him. Broken Tooth immediately rose and mounted her but a few seconds later, she snarled up at him and threw him off. It was a spectacular scene as they were mating in the shade of a flame of the forest tree, its red flowers carpeting the ground. The tigers mated every ten to twelve minutes until the sun set. The remnants of a sambar carcass floated in the water and crocodiles sniffed the edges. Broken Tooth snarled at them but did not have the energy to pursue them. The carcass kept the mating tigers rooted to the edge of the water. It was nearly 6.30 p.m. when Fateh left. He had watched the tigers mate eight times in eighty-eight minutes. It was the first time he had seen mating tigers. For Fateh, it remained one of the most important days of his life.

Young tigresses first come into oestrus between twenty-eight to thirty-six months. This is when conception can happen. Male tigers can father a litter from the age of forty to fifty months. A tigress who conceives may not come into oestrus again for eighteen to twenty-two months. If conception does not take place or if a litter is lost, she will come into oestrus in one to three months. Tigers are induced ovulators—the female releases her egg only when mating has begun. The male tiger has a bone in the penis that stimulates the tigress, inducing ovulation. The penis has penile spines that induce this process and cause pain to the tigress, who roars and tries to slap the male off her.

The sexual world of tigers is invisible to most and it was the same for me. I have been through endless books and journals but so little is described regarding this facet of the tiger's life. And especially in the wild! My very best observation had to do with a long courtship period that occurred in the mid-1980s between Noon and Broken Tooth. This is what I wrote nearly forty years ago. 'Every day we set out eagerly to search for evidence of the pair. Often we would find them together, either lying near each other or occasionally nuzzling each other. On one memorable occasion, they indulged in a mock boxing fight, rearing up on their hind legs to swat each other. Low growls resounded but at most, it was a playful engagement. As the days passed, the evenings were full of tiger sounds—long moans and roars. In the day, there was lots of marking and urinating by the female. The male responded with endless rounds of flehmen. The intensity of their interactions increased and each day we thought we would see them mating. After two weeks, I gave up and went to Delhi. It had been a long courtship and such long periods of courtship are seldom recorded.'

◆

For the tigress, use of her scent by marking and rubbing trees and bushes is a vital way to attract male tigers to her. The field of odour must be as large as possible and scent is generally sprayed on elevated spots. They are on walking trails and vehicle paths so that they are easily accessible for male tigers. The senses here are vital. The odour-detecting capacity of tigers is much higher than that of humans. Tigers can detect the scent of another tiger left on a tree or a bush or a scrape mark on the ground even when it is several days old. They glean large amounts of information from it. The Jacobson's organ, which I have mentioned earlier, is lined with receptor cells. Two tiny openings in the palate allow the scented air to reach the organ as the tiger inhales, and the nerves carry a message to the olfactory part of the brain, where the scent is analysed and identified. The sniffing behaviour is known as flehmen and the tiger curls back its upper lip, wrinkles its nose, and raises its head. This is vital in its ability to detect the oestrus cycle of the female. Glands that leave scent are around the anus and between the toes; sebaceous glands around the head, chin, lips, cheeks, and facial whiskers are also used to mark objects. Each tiger's scent is extremely individual. One tiger can decide to follow another based on what it might have detected in the scent. Sniffing the urine or smelling the anus all add to this cocktail of sexual interaction.

Sound is also used to attract male tigers. Sound, as I've mentioned earlier, is the tiger's most developed sense. The external ear flaps are like radar dishes and they pick up sounds from precisely where they originated. Low-frequency calls that are not audible to humans can also be picked up. The tiger has the ability to communicate by infrasound and this must be critical during the mating period both for males and females. Tigresses can walk for days across their home range, calling and scent-marking in their search for either resident or transient mates. Tigers roar much more during the mating period than at any other time. They forget about their normal lives in their effort to find a partner. The sex life of the tiger is about scent and sound, and both play a role in bringing the male and the female together. Every scent gland and vocal tract is at work, especially when reproductive reasons are triggered.

When a courting couple meet, they are very tactile. It is not just rubbing flanks and nuzzling with the occasional lick but also the touching and rubbing of cheeks. Sensitive whiskers serve a sensory function. They are twice as thick as the hair and rooted more deeply in the skin, in a capsule of blood. When a courting couple brush cheeks the whiskers carry signals to the brain and must play a vital role in arousal and copulation. The tiger's tongue is rough and rasping. A large number of minute, sharp, backward-pointing projections known as papillae cover their tongues. It is these rough surfaces that provoke sexual behaviour whenever the male and the female lick each other during mating. Oral sexual activity is known between tigers and both males and females lick each other's genitals and smell each other at the base of the tail. This helps in sexual stimulation.

While I watched them at close quarters, I found their eyes full of energy and electricity. They glowed and enhanced their facial expressions enormously. That look was a combination of tenderness and aggression.

In Ranthambhore, where there is a high density of tigers, males and females tend to spend six to ten days together during courting and mating. Again, there are always exceptions to this and I remember, in the mid-1980s, Broken Tooth following Noon around for more than three weeks waiting for her to become receptive. It was remarkable to watch how all the senses of the tiger are overactive in this period. But for most observers, this sexual life and behaviour of tigers have remained invisible.

My intimate contact with the sexual world of tigers involves two families of tigers, both of which were famous in Ranthambhore. T19 was the daughter of the famed tigress known as Machli or T16. The present century is full of stories of her and her legendary exploits. In February 2014, T19 gave birth to four cubs and a few months later, lost one of them, probably to a crocodile on the shores of Rajbagh palace.

In early 2017, the two daughters of T19—T83 and T84—popularly called Lightning and Arrowhead, were young adults and raring to go. Incessant aggression with their mother had forced her towards Lakarda and Semli some 5 kilometres away and both sisters were still fighting over the rights to their mother's territory, which was a prey-rich lake area. Arrowhead won the battle and her sister Lightning got pushed to the edge between Tamba Khan and Amaghati about 2 kilometres from the lakes. T19, their mother, was now in the Lakarda–Semli area with a new litter of three.

Amaghati faced the Sherpur valley and the villages. It was adjacent to where I then lived. This is where Lightning decided to remain in 2017. In the area of the lakes was a very shy male tiger. A recent arrival, T86 was only a few months older than both Lightning and Arrowhead. He kept himself away from human observation but was attracted equally to both Lightning and Arrowhead. He spent much of his time around the lakes with Arrowhead and she flirted endlessly with him and I knew that after or during the monsoon, they would mate.

Twice a week, he would stroll into the edges of Amaghati and Lightning would rub flanks and cheeks with him. I remember watching Lightning make all the moves to seduce him but he was reluctant—I thought that maybe she had not reached her oestrus. Both the sisters were getting ready to mate.

I left Ranthambhore just before the rains came and

returned in late October of 2017. When I assessed the information provided by the forest guards, it was clear that T86 had mated with both sisters. The question was if, at the age of forty-two to forty-three months, they were mature enough to have conceived. And could the young male at 3.9 years perform successfully? It was clear that their behaviour had changed and both sisters were not seen as frequently. Lightning would pass by the outer fringes once a week and Arrowhead was not as frequent around the lakes. I was certain that at least one was pregnant. But now, there was a new entrant to this story. An even younger male, T95, who was nearly three years old, was very active in the area and was actively trying to sniff out Lightning's movements. He was even occasionally making forays into T86's area of the lakes.

In mid-February of 2018, Arrowhead was spotted with three cubs about ten days old. T86 had done his job. She probably conceived in early November at the age of 3.6 years or so. Their eyes had barely opened.

A few days later, I received news of a tremendous battle that had taken place between two male tigers at Jogi Mahal. In between bouts of roaring, the tigers seemed to have inflicted injury on each other. When I got the information at midnight, I was sure it was T86 and T95 who had fought. Next morning, I watched both these male tigers lying still 10 metres from each other with T95 emitting continuous low growls. Here was one nearly three-year-old male fighting with a four-plus-year-old male. They looked totally exhausted. The forest guards at Jogi Mahal had been silenced by the fury of their roars for most of the night. T95 was bleeding on his right foreleg and T86 had gashes on his left foreleg. Thirty minutes after I arrived, T86 heaved himself up and with a severe limp, wandered slowly towards the Rajbagh palace. He sheltered in the palace for two days, nursing his wounds in the company of Arrowhead. She helped him by making a kill so they could feed. The intake of meat helps the recovery process.

A cool breeze blew and I watched the big male and his female companion sleeping in one of the chatris of this amazing palace. She was probably also licking his wounds. Her pugmarks were also at the site of the battle. It was clear she had watched the two males fight over her. T95 limped off to the edge of the park near the main entry gate. Scratched and bloody, he seemed to have lost this round. He nursed himself by much licking as saliva is the best antiseptic. This was my first ever sighting of the last stages of a major battle between two male tigers in Ranthambhore! I felt certain that Arrowhead had somehow triggered the conflict as only a few months earlier, both these male tigers were seen walking along the edge of the park, one behind the other, without any conflict. After a few days, all the tigers seemed to have settled back in place, and a calm descended, but Arrowhead had lost her cubs. Was this because of her negligence or had T95 played a role? The cubs were nowhere to be seen. Much more observation is required about this kind of conflict and its impacts. Why did the male tigers stop their fighting? Why were no fatal injuries inflicted? What is the role of the tigress? Did her presence help or hinder the process? And how did all of this impact her tiny cubs?

◆

As I have noted earlier, female tigers are induced ovulators, which means the actual act of mating, when the male inserts and withdraws his erect penis in the female, causes the release of an egg for fertilization. Therefore, several days of repeated mating are required to stimulate both the vagina and cervix and cause ovulation and guarantee the fertilization of the egg. This process might be influenced by the choice of mate and also the mating with more than one tiger during oestrus. I have known four tigresses that mated with two different male tigers at their time of oestrus. Can cubs of a single litter be fathered by more than one male as happens in cheetah society? We need more observations on this, but in my experience, this is indeed possible. In Ranthambhore, a tigress can spend four to nine days mating and if a second male is involved, then the period can get extended. The gestation period can be from 90 to 105 days though, in my experience in Ranthambhore, it tends to be around 100 days.

In the first week of June 2017, I found Lightning roaring away as she walked around her Amaghati area. By this time, T95 was also circling the edges and exploring Lightning's entire range. T86 was at his shyest self and using niches at the edge of the lakes to rest in. His favourite was a cave in the Kawaldar nallah. On 10 June, at 2 p.m., I was thrilled to find both T95 and Lightning in a small waterhole. They looked well fed and the male was cooling off in the water. Lightning looked restless. I instinctively knew she was coming into oestrus. Oestrus would probably last for five days but if she did not conceive her cycle could restart after twenty to twenty-five days. Now her oestrus cycle was starting within twelve to fifteen days of losing her last cub. That is how quickly the reproductive cycle can start.... Would I finally see at close quarters the incredible mating game?

A day later, on the way out of the park, I was

busy checking all the waterholes when suddenly, I saw Lightning and T95 lazing around in a pool of water. My heart thudded with joy. A dream was coming true.

I watched for an hour as Lightning tried her best to arouse the male by rubbing cheeks and flanks and nudging him, but, with a few snarls, he kept her at bay. She was not at the peak of her cycle. Dark clouds loomed on the horizon and soon a storm developed and the rain came crashing down. We had to flee for cover but when we returned an hour or two later, they had gone. I searched everywhere but the tigers had vanished. Would I see them again?

Each day I checked the water at Amaghati and on 12 June, I hit the jackpot. Let me explain here that in more than forty years of tiger-watching, I had never had a clear glimpse of mating tigers. Once, far away behind a bush, and another across a grassland were the closest I had ever got. Now, at a 25-foot radius around us, I had a pair of mating tigers. A very special dream of mine had come true. For over five hours, they mated fifteen times and the fastest frequency was thrice in ten minutes.

I could not believe it. How is the tiger able to copulate with this kind of frequency? I discussed this issue of the tiger's penis and its ability with Dharmendra Khandal, conservation biologist with Tiger Watch, and he was clear that it is because of the tiger's penis bone or baculum. All recent research has shown that this bone aids in quick copulation. Sliding a baculum bone in and out is much faster than waiting for blood to pump into tissues. Humans do not have this bone and mammals without them have larger erectile penises and much longer periods of copulation. The tiger's erection depends much more on the baculum than on tissue turgidity.

The tiger's penis is treasured in traditional Chinese medicine and used in soup, wine, or whisky as an aphrodisiac. In the Mekong River delta, a dried tiger penis with testicles still attached is placed in a bottle of wine or cognac and soaked for many weeks. As it matures, it is sipped every night! The tiger's baculum bone is used as an ornament for good luck and virility. Any form of consumption of this penis is supposed to be effective treatment for erectile dysfunction and thousands of dollars are spent in finding a tiger penis! These are the crazy ways that humans find to solve their problems. The demand for the penis and its bone has threatened the tiger's survival. Thoughts of the horrors of the illegal trade of the tiger's penis flashed across my mind as I watched Lightning. Love, aggression, cuddling, and the frantic ability of the female to continuously arouse the male into action is why the tigress is sometimes called a sex maniac! T95 and Lightning engaged in every position for the camera with low, rough growls. Once, the male turned on me with extreme aggression. They never left the waterhole. In between bouts of mating, the female would roll on her back and on approaching the male, lick him and nibble at him in an effort to arouse him. The female would then position herself seductively, making it clear she was ready for copulation.

When the male disengages after insertion, the female swings around explosively to slap him and he sidesteps or jumps away in response; this moment is mesmeric. So is the way he grips the scruff of her neck while mating. It prevents her from swivelling around and slapping him. As he catches the folds of skin on the neck, it tends to immobilize the tigress. This is also how the tigress carries her newly born cubs. The hold on the folds of skin on the neck is firm but gentle. When he exits the female after copulation, he jumps away rapidly; in fact, leaps off fearing a slap from the female, who, in those seconds, feels the sharp bristles of the penis raking her vaginal wall. The male fears a slash of her sharp claws. A tiger's claws can take the face off a human in one swipe and each claw can be 4 inches long. The tiger copulates in such a way that his weight does not squash the tigress. What the female does have to put up with is the tiger's rough and bristly penis that has spines on it and hurts on the way in, triggering her aggression.

I think what my son Hamir and I saw that day will remain etched on our minds forever. We were alone amidst the magic of tiger sounds and visuals as the sun danced off the courting tigers. The perfect setting for human observers. Had Lightning finally found her perfect mate? Time would tell. Both sisters could produce new litters by the end of the monsoon. The seeds of another generation of tigers were about to germinate.

7

THE SOCIAL LIFE OF TIGERS

*O*ne of the things I'd always wanted to see was a tigress with cubs aged between one and four months, so as to observe the bonding between mother and cubs. We had seen Noon's cubs at five months but the earlier period was altogether invisible. Laxmi would grant us a peek into this stage of a tiger's life. In the early 1980s, she had moved to a corner of her mother Padmini's range between Lakarda and Bakaula, encompassing the valley of Semli. In the first part of the 1980s, she was evasive and elusive. I believe this was her basic nature as she had grown up in an environment that was heavily disturbed by humans.

However, early one morning in March 1986, when Laxmi was nearly ten years old, she gave me the privilege of observing her with her young cubs—an experience that would grant me more insight into the mysterious world of tigers. That day, as I turned a bend in the road, there facing me at the edge of the track was Laxmi. She sat very still, looking at me. At first, I did not see what was around her. Then I realized that three tiny cubs were peeping around a bush. I froze. Soon, she relaxed and all three cubs came out to cuddle her. She licked them vigorously. The cubs looked about two months old. It seemed that this was their first encounter with a jeep. As she licked her cubs, I realized that another aspect of the tiger's secret life was unfolding before my very eyes. The cubs slowly found her teats and she lay back to suckle them. This was, for me, a first. Their tiny feet pushed away at her belly, stimulating the flow of milk, as they suckled furiously. After ten minutes, they jumped around her head and stalked a butterfly in the grass. One of them jumped on her back and another pulled at her tail while she licked the third cub. I watched this family drama for a half-hour. Tears rolled down my cheeks as a tangle of emotions exploded within. I had seen all manner of tiger behaviour in the course of my life with the wild animal. I had seen the kills. I had seen how they ate. I had seen the aggression, the power, and the fierceness. Here I was witnessing the tender care, the devotion, and a mother's love. Gentle and loving, the tigress soon rose and led her cubs away. For the next three months, it was their remarkable family life that completely captivated me. Laxmi was very much like Padmini in her basic temperament. Calm and mature-looking, I seldom saw her ruffled. She had a lovely deep colour to her coat, and a swagger as she walked the paths and roads. She never feared the resident male or even transients. She commanded respect. Nothing she did was reckless or risky—and underneath it all was the fact that she was an amazingly devoted mother.

The next morning I found Laxmi sitting in a grass patch 10 to 15 metres from the jeep track. Her three cubs surrounded her. One nuzzled her face, another rested against her back, the third watched us curiously. Very tentatively, one of the cubs moved a little towards us before rushing back to the security of its mother. Soon, the cubs turned to each other and began leaping into the air and knocking into each other. After every bout, they rushed to Laxmi, who licked and cuddled them and soon decided to lie on her side and suckle them. All three soon found a teat and began to feed. I watched this remarkable spectacle for more than fifteen minutes. I have never seen such a display of love and warmth, such evidence of the strong bonding between a tigress and her cubs.

Over the next few days, we encountered Laxmi's family regularly in the valley of Semli and after each encounter, we were able to get closer and closer. Laxmi slowly got used to us. After that she was never bothered by our presence or our cameras clicking away. Slowly, the cubs got bolder and one of them—who was the most confident—even approached within one metre of our jeep. We soon realized that there were two females and one male cub.

One afternoon I found Laxmi just after she had killed a chital stag. She dragged it quickly up the rise of a hill and into thicker forest. Of the cubs there was no sign. In about ten minutes, she came out of the forest and walked 100 metres towards a network of ravines. I decided to follow, taking the jeep off-track and cross-country. Laxmi approached a bend in the ravine and called out 'Aaooo' several times. As she turned the bend, I drove to the edge of the hill to look down. Below us was a gorge 30 metres long and 10 metres wide, surrounded on two sides by a cliff and a rock overhang some 20 metres high. There were two caves in the cliff face and the three cubs came rushing out of one of them. Dense cover carpeted the floor of the gorge and a large pool of water reflected the light of the evening sun. It was a perfect hideout. Amidst a great deal of squeaking and squalling, the cubs greeted their mother with much nuzzling and slowly followed her out of the ravine, meowing plaintively, as if they knew they were being led to a feast. On reaching a clearing, Laxmi settled down to lick her cubs, showing once again the intimate bond they shared. They then strode off towards where the carcass had been left. I followed through bush and rock until I could go no further. As I watched through a pair of binoculars, I noticed that Laxmi had opened the rump of the spotted deer and the cubs were greedily devouring whatever they could. It was clear that the cubs were used to meat even before the age of three months. It is this diet of milk and meat that makes them grow so quickly. Adult tigers prefer to eat from the choicest portion of the carcass, which is the rump, and then slowly move towards the neck. Cubs, in their greed, attack whichever portion they get to first. While they eat they snarl, hiss, and try to growl. It is incredible, the variety that exists in the language of the tiger.

For the next few weeks, Fateh and I spent many days watching the cubs, observing and documenting facets of their lives and recording events that we had never seen before. It was April and the onset of summer. While waiting for Laxmi the cubs spent much of their time soaking in the water and fighting the heat. Cooling off in water is essential when summer temperatures cross 40 °C to 45 °C.

For Laxmi's young family, a bit of playing, some climbing and exploring, and a lot of sleeping was their daily routine. Laxmi's days were spent searching for prey. Choosing the right bush, she would appear to be asleep but at the slightest sound, she would be alert and ready to pounce on an unsuspecting deer. Several times we watched her bring portions of her kill to the cubs to feed on. Whenever this happened, the cubs would bound towards her in great excitement, each trying to be the first to reach the kill. The cubs were now becoming more adventurous, exploring the small ravine which was their den, nibbling at twigs and branches, chasing partridges and hares, chewing whatever came their way, prodding at stones and boulders, and investigating any small movement, be it of birds or even lizards. New sounds like the sudden booming alarm call of the sambar, which had frightened them earlier, would now be accepted and they would raise their heads to sniff the air. The raucous barking of a troop of langurs would keep them alert and motionless and the shrill call of the stork-billed kingfisher would arouse their curiosity. A whole new world of sight and sound was unfolding and these young ones were learning to interpret it. The remnants of bones around their den would attract a stream of king vultures and crows and their movement was carefully watched by the cubs. The vultures never tried to land as the gorge was too narrow for them to feel safe. Crows were chased away. The occasional mongoose that slipped into the ravine would quickly retreat because the smell of tigers was everywhere.

We also noticed the regular presence of a big male within these ravines. Could it be the male that fathered the litter? Did the male play a role in bringing up the cubs? In a few weeks we had our most startling revelations. Up until then, there were no records that we were aware of that showed the presence of the male tiger in the first days after the cubs were born. It is a time when the tigress chooses the thickest area in which to deliver her cubs. Giving birth is a long, difficult, and arduous process as she can deliver up to seven cubs. Complete devotion of the tigress to her cubs in the first days ensures their safety, but seeing the father with the young cubs was a dream fulfilled.

This was the same period of time during which Noon had her first litter and Nalghati her second. I was at times lucky enough to see all the families in one day and draw fascinating comparisons. But we still were not able to record the role of the father figure. For a long time it was presumed that male tigers were a threat to young cubs and frequently killed them. Most believed that there was no father figure in the tiger family. I assumed this to be true also. But an encounter in the valley of Bakaula changed all that.

Bakaula was the coolest place in the park. Full of water and thick green jamun groves, it was a favourite resting place for tigers in the day and especially in the summer. This is where President Clinton saw two tigers on his visit to Ranthambhore. The scenery around here is quite spectacular. Cliffs rise up around the water and it is a great place to watch both Bonelli's eagles and stork-billed kingfishers. I would spend many hours in the summer exploring it and it was here that Fateh's son, Goverdhan, and his companions witnessed an amazing interaction between a tiger and a leopard. Looking for beehives in the trees, they suddenly spotted a leopard atop the branches. She appeared bothered and restless, and looking around, they found a young sub-adult up another tree across the nullah. The cub appeared even more restless, moving up and down the branches and nervously looking down. The leopardess called to her cub several times. The green bushes hid the fact that there was a tiger sitting at the base of the tree that the leopard had climbed. The cub could not contain its fright and started sliding down the tree, urinating in absolute panic. Within seconds of it descending the tree, there was a huge growl and sounds of splashing water. A peacock cried out in alarm and took off. Then an ominous silence fell before Goverdhan and his companions saw the tiger sprawled over the carcass of the young leopard. The leopardess looked on helplessly from the safety of her tree, as the tiger started eating and cracking the bones. It was another unique encounter that Ranthambhore had provided.

In the 1980s, I spent a lot of time in Bakaula. After the lakes, it was one of my favourite spots. If the lakes were very open, Bakaula was thick and green and cool. In the summer it was like an air-conditioned room. This is a spectacular time in the forest as the flame of the forest blooms. The tree turns a startling red, the ground beneath the trees is littered with fallen flowers, and entire stretches of Bakaula, Kachida, and Anantpura turn crimson. It was here in this red and green mosaic of forest that another window in the family life of tigers opened for me.

It was 1 May 1986. At the edge of Semli, in the gorge of Bakaula, Fateh came across the Bakaula male and Laxmi. They were sitting on the vehicle track, facing each other. On both sides of the track were thick groves of jamun, cool, lush, and green. The temperature was nearing 45 °C. The area around was dotted with pools of water. Laxmi rose briefly and nuzzled the male and then flopped on the edge of the track a few metres away. A pair of Bonelli's eagles circled above a cliff where they nested. I heard the chatter of a stork-billed kingfisher. Suddenly, this tranquil scene was disturbed by the sound of a rolling pebble. Both tigers were immediately alert. Laxmi moved cautiously towards the sound and the male had his head up. A sambar's alarm call echoed across the gorge. Laxmi had been spotted and a sambar walked away up an incline with its tail up. Laxmi was too far off to attack, but the sambar's path was closer to the Bakaula male. He was crouched, muscles rippling, as the sambar approached. She was not expecting a second tiger. In a flash, the male took off. Six bounds and he was on the sambar, forcing it down and quickly gripping its throat. From around the corner, a jeep full of chattering tourists approached the big male who was in the process of choking the sambar. Surprised, he took cover behind a bush. The sambar was not dead and twitched with small spasms. Laxmi, who was not shy of jeeps, quickly approached and provided the finishing touches and began the tedious process of dragging the 180-kilogram carcass to thicker cover. The male watched alertly as Laxmi reached a small clearing. The tiger moved towards her and Fateh watched a spectacular tug of war. The male had a grip on the rump and pulled at the hind leg, while Laxmi, at the neck, pulled in the other direction. The carcass was stretched between them, the tug of war interspersed with vicious, low-pitched growls and snarls. Then, suddenly, with a

Herculean effort, Laxmi pulled the whole body and the male several metres. Pulling nearly 450 kilograms left her exhausted and she released her grip, leaving the male to drag the sambar away. Laxmi strode off to Semli and the den where her cubs lay. She emitted a low rolling call and was answered by bird-like squeaks from her four-month-old cubs. After much licking and cuddling with endless squeaks, purrs, and grunts, she led her cubs back and they must have known they were going to a feast as they circled her and jumped around her flanks. As they walked, they clambered up branches of trees and romped around joyously. Laxmi was taking them to the male tiger. Clearly, this was not the first time they were going to share a kill with their father. They soon vanished into the bushes. This remarkable encounter was also responsible for dispelling the belief that male tigers killed their cubs, especially in the first months of their lives. Yet again, the tigers of Ranthambhore were rewriting the natural history of tigers.

Laxmi had opened up a wealth of information on the early family life of tigers and some of our pictures were the first ever of both male and female with cubs. We had now seen and recorded evidence of the big male as a father figure. Our observations in the 1980s then took on a completely different dimension a few years ago as yet another chapter was added to the natural history of the tiger. A tigress had died, probably of natural causes, leaving behind two three-month-old female cubs. The park management decided to hand-feed them in the wild. While doing this, they noticed that every few days a big male's pugmarks would appear and for a day or so, the cubs seemed to engage with him. The father kept an eye on these cubs until they were twenty-two months old, allowing them to share his food and walk with him while he patrolled. Big male tigers in the role of mother! When the two females were finally sent to Sariska because they were becoming a nuisance in the buffer area of the park, preying on livestock, the big male roared for most of the night trying to find them.

This event repeated itself when another tigress vanished, leaving three little cubs behind. Here, the big male did much the same. Even after they were grown up, the three-year-old male cubs would band together and follow the father around. I believe extreme events or extenuating circumstances can result in new patterns of behaviour and this is what some of Ranthambhore's tigers revealed.

Depending on the circumstances, it is quite clear that tigers can band together to survive even if they are males. These are temporary coalitions. Usually, the male tiger's territory encompasses the home ranges of several tigresses and while patrolling his terrain, he is likely to encounter them and even spend time sharing kills and relaxing. He could also have fathered more than one litter in his range. It is only when a transient male enters that the tigress and her cubs feel threatened.

As Laxmi's cubs grew, we had many encounters with them. We observed the different stages of family life, especially the dominance of the cubs over each other and the strict hierarchy each sibling observed in relation to the other. One of my final glimpses of this family was when they were sixteen months old. Late one afternoon, we found all the siblings at the Semli waterhole. They seemed to be anxiously waiting for the arrival of their mother. It looked as if she had been away for most of the day. After an hour, the dominant male cub suddenly became alert and in minutes, Laxmi appeared from behind the bushes. In a flash, the cubs— now nearly her size—rushed to cuddle and rub flanks and then started the most amazing purring I have ever heard. This was the big greeting after a long absence as the cubs and their mother bonded. The purring was louder than anything you could hear on Bose speakers. For me, it was a truly memorable day so far as tiger sounds were concerned. My senses were overwhelmed.

I could not hear the driver speak, that's how loud the purring was. After nearly twenty minutes, all four sat around the waterhole ready to start another night. At 6 p.m., a group of chital approached the waterhole, to quench their thirst. The cubs froze in their positions and Laxmi was fully alert. The chital had not seen the tigers. Their tails were up but on suspicion only. They were desperate to get to the water to drink. One step at a time, they walked slowly towards the water in between Laxmi and her startled cubs. With her head down, Laxmi seemed to glide like a snake for a few metres, and then one of the deer spotted her and an alarm call resounded, sending all the deer into a panic. Each tiger exploded into action. In the chaos and confusion, a fawn became separated from its mother and headed in Laxmi's direction. In one leap, Laxmi pinioned the fawn between her paws and grabbed the back of the neck. The poor deer squeaked and died. A stork-billed kingfisher took off from his perch, his blue wings glinting in the fading light. Picking up the fawn, Laxmi carried it a few metres away, followed greedily by all her cubs. She then dropped the fawn to the ground and sprawled on top of it. The fawn was barely visible below her body as she snarled at her approaching cubs. The dominant male cub settled in front of her, snarling back. Another female cub also settled next to her sibling. Then both cubs started a moaning sound like a never-ending howl. I had never heard this sound before. They appeared to be begging, but Laxmi snarled viciously at them and lifted the tiny carcass a few metres further. Now all the cubs were moaning non-stop. This went on for several minutes until two of the cubs decided to leap at their mother and cannonball her off the carcass. She moved off and the male cub snatched away the fawn and, in seconds, was behind a bush devouring it. There is no sharing at this age and the rest watched for forty-five minutes as he ate. When he was done he abandoned the carcass and began to eat grass. Many tigers do this in an effort to help digestion or to bring up furballs. It is a form of self-medication. In some cases, the eating of grass helps to rid the intestines of parasites and worms. It was nearly dark when they all moved off down the road.

By now, I had witnessed the early stages of semi-independence and a remarkable evening of vocalizations. It had been a most productive day in terms of sound and bonding. Tigers are not very vocal as a rule. Their low, haunting roar echoing far and wide means either that big males are sounding out their territories and signalling to each other or females are in oestrus attracting a male. When tigresses have young cubs, they tend to squeak to each other in order not to attract attention. It is a bird-like sound and sometimes difficult to assess as a tiger sound.

It is around the age of eighteen months that the first detachment in the relationship between mother and cubs occurs. This is also the time when the cubs get their permanent teeth. The tigress forces the process, ensuring that her cubs are well prepared for their solitary existence in the future. Laxmi's cubs had started becoming more aggressive with each other now. This was especially true of the two females. Laxmi's absences grew longer but she would still lead her cubs to the kill. It was while she was absent that the two females would become really aggressive, circling each other and then suddenly rearing up on their hind legs to box each other or hiss viciously. The smaller of the females would normally submit by rolling over on her back. The male cub was now spending much time with the smaller female. I knew instinctively that the larger female would be the first to leave. Even Laxmi was less tolerant of her larger female cub. The young tigers were beginning to assert their highly individualistic characteristics. The father, the big Bakaula male, continued to interact with the family but now the big male cub would keep his distance. My last sighting of all three cubs together was soon after they were twenty months old. It was late one evening in June. I found all three cubs lazing around the Semli waterhole. Of Laxmi there was no sign. Suddenly a sambar hind appeared from the rear with two young ones. The three tigers crawled into different positions as if ready to attack and then charged at the deer. Within seconds they were out of sight in thicker forest. I moved the jeep around and discovered the male cub choking one of the younger deer, who flicked its tail a few times and died. It was the first successful kill by the cubs that I had witnessed, with all three working as a team. This is the final lesson in independence and I knew the male would soon be on his way. The break-up of the family would start soon. The youngest female would be the last to go.

8

THE TIGER IN INDIA AND THE WORLD

The tiger in India has fared well. There is no question about this. In fact, this has been a very pleasant surprise for me. In the late 1990s, I thought that by the turn of the century, most of India's tigers would be wiped out, but it did not happen. As I have said, I am in my fiftieth year of tiger-watching. India still has about 2,500 to 3,000 tigers in pockets of habitat across the land. Given that this same land has to support nearly 1.4 billion people, whom tigers have to coexist with, this is a remarkable feat. It is the result of some very hard work by some committed government officers and some passionate non-governmental partners. Yes, there is a lot of room for improvement and the management strategies are shoddy most of the time. One of the problems that arises occasionally, and did so recently in Ranthambhore, for example, is conflict between humans and tigers. In May 2025, a tigress called Kankati, the daughter of the tigress called Arrowhead, whom we have met in these pages, claimed her second human victim, a park ranger. Kankati and several other tigers had lost their fear of humans because they had grown accustomed to being fed with live bait and were turning into 'semi-domesticated animals waiting to be fed' in the words of Dharmendra

Khandal (*Indian Express*, 13 May 2025). Inevitably, this over-familiarity with humans had tragic consequences with a tiger turning man-killer. In such circumstances, my view is clear. Immediate steps should be taken by the authorities to stop whatever practices have led to the tragedy and the guilty tiger cannot be allowed to roam free. Some tigers become nasty killers and must be imprisoned just like humans are for murder. That is really the only way that man and tiger will be able to survive into the future.

Such unfortunate developments aside, what does need to be celebrated is the fact that we have managed to make wild tigers thrive in our country. A miracle!

The rest of the world has not done as well and tiger populations have dwindled drastically across Asia and all tiger-range states. There is little political will to conserve them and priorities have changed. India now holds more than 75 per cent of the world's tigers. That in itself is incredible. I would never have imagined it possible when I first began watching tigers.

As I come to the end of this short book, my head is full of tiger encounters. They never leave you. I remember each one as if it took place yesterday. And many have not just been memorable but extraordinary. My most memorable encounter took place in November 2024. I was following the resident tigress of the lakes and her three seventeen-month-old sub-adult cubs. As they walked the edges of the lake, one of them suddenly stopped. He gingerly looked at the grass below and suddenly all four tigers seemed to surround a spot and lunged forward and backward. I knew it was a snake. They were being careful of its fangs. Mom then watched as the cubs dealt with a 12-foot python. The python put up an enormous fight but it was all in vain. The male cub finally got a good grip on it, pulled it out from where it was sheltering, and the snake was then killed. All four tigers then fed on it in the grass for three hours—a good 25- to 30-kilogram feast.

I could not believe it. A dream come true. It had taken forty-nine years but I had the first real photo record of such an encounter in the world. My wife filmed it. Heaven!

How did we manage to keep this magical animal alive? I think it has to be because of the mindset of our people and their traditional beliefs that gave a special sanctity to the tiger. It was the vehicle of the goddess who brought good fortune and defeated evil. Even if some poachers went after the tiger, many kept away from this dastardly act. It was against their beliefs. The tiger for many of our people was regarded as sacred, a divine creature, and it is deeply embedded in the myth, legend, and beliefs of our people. This has played the most critical role in keeping it alive.

Ancient Indian and South Asian history is full of tigers, of course, but an enormous cult of the tiger arose across the rest of Asia as well, including parts of Siberia. The tiger became an integral part of the life of traditional communities, and its influence on religious cults and legends, on art and literature, and on a widespread way of life was unmatched by any other non-domesticated animal. Wherever it existed, it left its impression on the psyche of the people. The Warli tribal gods existed because of the animal. Phallus-shaped wooden and stone images of the tiger, often daubed in red to indicate their extreme sanctity, were placed everywhere as symbols of fertility, not just for crops but also for marriage and the birth of children. There were festivals dedicated to the tiger god all across India, and there were frequent ritualistic dances in which dancers painted themselves with tiger stripes and then propitiated the tiger god. The tiger commanded great fear and respect across different religions. A legend of a compassionate prince giving his body to save the life of a starving tigress and her cubs is found in several sacred Buddhist texts.

Thousands of miles away in Siberia, the Udege tribal people also honoured the tiger as their god. To the Udege, the tiger is the spirit of the taiga (evergreen forests) and guardian of the trees and mountains, a divine force of nature. Similarly, many Koreans still believe that their land is blessed by the blue dragon and the white tiger, and that the image of the tiger repels evil spirits and protects people's fortunes. Much the same was felt in China. Many believe that the tiger first originated in China and then spread across Asia. At one time, most Chinese believed that the breath of the tiger created the wind. Edward Schafer in his book, *The Vermilion Bird* (1967), states, 'Chinese literature from the earliest times is full of tiger stories—man-eating tigers, were-tigers, symbolic tigers, anti-tiger spells, tiger hunts—tigers in China are like mice in a cheese factory.' Three thousand years ago, during the Shang dynasty, people in the Shaanxi province believed that the tigers symbolized regeneration. A bride would receive two dough tigers when she first arrived at her husband's house (a tradition that continues to this day). In Chinese medicine, the body of the tiger was believed to hold miraculous cures. Nearly any kind of disease could be overcome by 'eating the tiger'. Tribal communities believed that the white tiger was a part of the Milky Way and from there he protected the earth. Just as the goddess Durga rides a tiger in her attempt to defeat evil, the Taoist leader in China is shown riding a tiger in his search for a dragon-tiger elixir for eternal life. Indeed, the parallels in tiger belief between China and India are extraordinary.

Tigers were also a symbol of power in China, and their image conferred both strength and courage. The male tiger, as the god of war, was responsible for fighting demons. Chinese soldiers dressed in imitation tiger skins with tails for protection. The tiger was the guardian of China, the protector against evil, and the protector of the living and the dead. Tiger-striped pillows still keep away nightmares, and children don tiger-patterned hats, collars, and shoes to keep away evil. The richness of tiger symbolism in China has no equivalent in the belief systems of Christian Europe.

Wherever the tiger lived, its cult enveloped people. In the forests of Vietnam, Laos, and Cambodia, the tribals believed that the tiger was first among animals and had intense supernatural powers, including the ability to transform into a human being. Mnong tribals from the region, much like the Warlis in India, connected the worship of the tiger to the worship of grain, and they believed this resulted in rich harvests from fertile soil. All across Malaysia and Indonesia, people believed in the tiger shaman who could evoke the tiger and then perform miraculous cures on any patient's body in order to repel sickness and disease. They also believed in were-tigers or spirit-people who can change into tigers and then back into humans. Were-tigers were protective spirits who kept a link between the past and the present, as for most forest people, the souls of ancestors were thought to reside in the tiger. The cult of the tiger linked beliefs throughout the land of the tiger, from the Manchurian taiga to the Indian forest and the Sumatran jungle.

More than 1 billion people live in twenty-first-century India. It also boasts nearly half the world's tiger population, half the world's Asiatic elephant population, and an array of other living creatures. One might argue that these animal populations might not have survived at all if these people had not maintained a core belief in nature's power. The Asiatic elephant invoked the spectre of Ganesha, the elephant god; the tiger was the vehicle of Durga.

The future of the tiger around the world today hangs in the balance. We have done a good job of conserving the tiger in India but both here and elsewhere, over the next decade, it's imperative that government and non-governmental experts partner in genuine ways to manage wild tiger populations. We might be able to turn the situation around. Will it happen? I certainly hope so, though it will be tough for leaders across the world to make common cause where tiger conservation is concerned, given the current levels of mistrust between countries. But what the world cannot ignore is the fact that there is nothing more important than protecting tiger habitats and keeping tigers alive. When you protect tigers, you protect the entire habitat, down to the smallest insect. There is no better way to minimize the impact of global warming or climate change.

The great vehicle of the goddess deserves our very best commitment. I hope younger generations will commit themselves fully to the battle to save wild tigers. I have done so for five decades, along with numerous others who dedicated their lives to the cause, and I hope that level of commitment will continue. I have had the extraordinary privilege of seeing nearly 200 different tigers in the wild and every one of them lit up my life with unimaginable brilliance. I hope more and more people will experience this magnificent animal as I have and do everything in their power to ensure it does not vanish off the face of the earth.

www.ingramcontent.com/pod-product-compliance
Lightning Source LLC
Chambersburg PA
CBHW051728260326
41914CB00040B/2010/J